12 13 14 15 16 17 18 19 20

Note to Parents

The Great 123 Search is a wonderful book to help children learn their numbers. It is designed for those children just learning their 123's, as well as older children who are becoming familiar with applying what they already know.

The 123 fun begins with the cover of this book, which contains 20 different groups of objects for children to count. For instance, children can count one rhinoceros horn, two elephant tusks, and three ladybugs, all the way to nineteen dots on the dice and twenty fingers and toes on the monkey. Let your child count each set of objects and tell you how many there are in each group. This little exercise will help you decide whether to start your child with just mastering each number or to offer the challenge of turning the pages of the book and counting all the objects to be found.

Each spread is filled with a particular number of various items. While some objects in the scene will be easy to find and count by children, others are hidden. Children will also be introduced to a basic addition equation for each number presented. You and your child will be able to share this book again and again, finding and counting new objects each time. When your child thinks everything has been found, turn to the answer key at the end of the book and check!

To my dad, Stanley Curtis
—A. T. J.

To my parents and especially Beth
—D. L.

Copyright © 1991 RGA Publishing Group, Inc. All rights reserved.

ISBN: 1-56288-118-3 Library of Congress Catalog Card Number: 91-73087
Printed in U.S.A.   0 9 8 7 6 5 4 3 2 1

Published by Checkerboard Press, Inc.
30 Vesey Street, New York, NY 10007

The GREAT 123 Search

By Anna T. Johannson
Illustrated by Dave Lowe

CHECKERBOARD PRESS
New York

1, 2

This empty cage is missing one amusing kangaroo,
And one baboon has lost its mate—just find her in this zoo!

$0 + $  $= 1$  $+ $  $= 2$

3 Two playful monkeys in the jungle swung from tree to tree.
Can you find a little friend for them to make the twosome three?
+ = 3

4 Three naughty little kittens played a goofy game of chase!
Now they're hiding from their mommy—can you find them in this place?

🐱 + 🐱🐱🐱 = 4

5 The captain of a pirate ship uncovered buried gold.
Can you find four other treasure chests this island scene may hold?

🧰 + 🧰🧰🧰 = 5

6 The neighbor's puppy buried bones around an apple tree.
There are five more bones in this yard—how many do you see?

🦴 + 🦴🦴🦴🦴🦴 = 6

7

The seven circus kangaroos are doing silly tricks.
There's one who's standing on his head—where are the other six?

8 On a roller coaster ride a hippo took his teddy bear.
Can you find his seven furry friends that might be anywhere?

🐻 + 🐻🐻🐻🐻🐻🐻 = 8

9

A mermaid looked for pretty shells along the ocean floor.
She found one lying on the sand—please help her find eight more!

+ = 9

10 A duckling lost his rubber boot while playing in the snow.
Nine other boots are missing, too—where are they, do you know?

1 + 9 = 10

11 On a windy afternoon some piglets flew their kite up high.
You'll find ten other hidden kites on land and in the sky!

◇ + ◈ ◊ ◇ ◇ ▥ ◇ ◈ ▦ ◇ ◆ = 11

SALE

$12.00

12

A bashful skunk bought perfume from a bunny at the mall.
Eleven other bunnies hide—just try to count them all!

🐰 + 🐰🐰🐰🐰🐰🐰🐰🐰🐰🐰🐰 = 12

13 A hairy ape munched on some fruit while visiting the fair.
There are at least twelve more bananas hidden everywhere!

🍌 + 🍌🍌🍌🍌🍌🍌🍌🍌🍌🍌🍌🍌 = **13**

14

In a corner of the library, a bookworm gnawed a book.
You may see thirteen others, too, if on this page you look!

🐛 + 🐛🐛🐛🐛🐛🐛🐛🐛🐛🐛🐛🐛🐛 = 14

15

One blazing summer day a lizard floated in a pool.
Can you find his fourteen buddies who are trying to stay cool?

🦎 + 🐾🐾🐾🐾🐾🐾🐾🐾🐾🐾🐾🐾🐾🐾 = 15

16

The nervous pitcher inched his way up to the baseball mound.
Find fifteen more balls on this field—how many have you found?

⚾ + ⚾⚾⚾⚾⚾⚾⚾⚾⚾⚾⚾⚾⚾⚾⚾ = 16

17 A shipwrecked parrot crawled ashore an island paradise.
He needs to find his sixteen friends to make this scene quite nice!

18 A Scout got lost while hiking when he stopped to pull his socks. Find seventeen more Cub Scouts who are hiding in these rocks!

👦 + 🧑🧑🧑🧑🧑🧑🧑🧑🧑🧑🧑🧑🧑🧑🧑🧑🧑 =18

19 A chimp rode on a skateboard with a one-eyed kangaroo.
Can you believe that eighteen skateboards hide here just for you?

🛹 + 🛹🛹🛹🛹🛹🛹🛹🛹🛹🛹🛹🛹🛹🛹🛹🛹🛹 = 19

20

A little kitten wished upon a star that shined so bright.
Please try and help find nineteen more, then wish her a good night!

☆ + ☆☆☆☆☆☆☆☆☆☆☆☆☆☆☆☆☆☆☆ = **20**

Answers

Cover: 1 rhinoceros horn, 2 elephant tusks, 3 ladybugs, 4 cloverleafs, 5 feathers on bird's head, 6 eggs, 7 pool balls, 8 arms on octopus, 9 of Hearts (card), 10 legs on caterpillar, 11 candles and 11 flowers on birthday cake, 12 teeth on rhinoceros, 13 dots on monkey's shorts, 14 eyelashes on elephant, 15 ribs on monkey's waistband, 16 cookies, 17 yellow segments on caterpillar, 18 inches on ruler, 19 dots on dice, 20 fingers and toes on monkey

1,2: 1, 1 arrow, 1 bird, 1 camera, 1 cup, 1 girl, 1 handkerchief, 1 kangaroo, 1 key, 1 man, 1 old lady, 1 old man, 1 purse, 1 squirrel, 1 tie, 2, 2 baboons, 2 balloons, 2 bows, 2 boys, 2 bracelets, 2 cages, 2 feathers on bird's head, 2 giraffes, 2 holes in man's hat, 2 nuts, 2 pillows, 2 pockets, 2 ponytails, 2 rings, 2 rope loops around upper ring, 2 straws, 2 tail feathers, 2 tall trees, 2 tears, 2 watches

3: 3, 3 bananas in monkey's hand, 3 birds, 3 bunches of bananas, 3 butterflies, 3 cans in backpack, 3 coconuts, 3 holes in explorer's hat, 3 monkeys, 3 patches on pant leg, 3 shoelace loops, 3 smoke rings, 3 stripes on each of 3 birds' bills, 3 tail loops around branch, 3 teeth on each stone tiger

4: 4, 4 arms on statue, 4 birds, 4 books, 4 buttons on chair, 4 buttons on coat, 4 cats, 4 chair legs, 4 drawers, 4 eyes in picture, 4 fingers in picture, 4 flowers, 4 light bulbs, 4 light switches, 4 magazines, 4 medals, 4 mice, 4 petals on each of 4 flowers, 4 pictures, 4 rings in rug, 4 spots on pillow, 4 stripes on flowerpot, 4 stripes on each of 2 pillows, 4 table legs, 4 toes on each of 4 birds, 4 trees, 4 windowpanes in 1 window

5: 5, 5 bracelets on pirate, 5 buttons on captain's sleeve, 5 feathers on 1 parrot wing, 5 fringes on sash, 5 fronds on palm tree, 5 goblets, 5 legs on hermit crab, 5 pirates, 5 sails, 5 shark fins, 5 teeth on 1 pirate, 5 treasure chests

6: 6, 6 acorns, 6 apples, 6 birds, 6 bones, 6 mice, 6 mushrooms, 6 spokes on each of 2 wheels, 6 toes on each sitting bird, 6 wheels, 6 windowpanes on yellow house, 6 windows on red house, 6 yellow sideboards on house

7: 7, 7 balloons, 7 buttons on ringmaster's shirt, 7 dots on clown, 7 drops of water, 7 hippos, 7 juggling hoops, 7 kangaroos, 7 penguins, 7 spokes on unicycle, 7 stripes on bird bill, 7 stripes on popcorn vendor's hat, 7 teeth on gorilla, 7 toes on weight lifter, 7 triangles on stilt walker's leg

8: 8, 8 balloons, 8 dots on hippo's shirt, 8 flamingos, 8 green train cars, 8 prongs on moose's antlers, 8 purple train cars, 8 roller coaster trains, 8 teddy bears, 8 toes on hippos, 8 toes on panda, 8 triangles on hippo's shirt, 8 wheels on purple train, 8 wheels on red train, 8 whiskers on hippo

9: 9, 9 air bubbles, 9 arms on coral, 9 boards on boat, 9 fish, 9 fishermen, 9 fishing poles, 9 links on anchor chain, 9 people on beach, 9 rocks on coast, 9 sea gulls, 9 seashells, 9 seaweed branches, 9 segments on mermaid's tail fin, 9 starfish, 9 starfish arms, 9 worms on fishhook

10: 10, 10 animals, 10 branches, 10 buttons, 10 feathers on 1 duck's wing, 10 fringes on each end of green scarf, 10 ribs around green hat, 10 rubber boots, 10 scarves, 10 snowballs, 10 spots on scarf, 10 stripes on duck's shirt

11: 11, 11 bees, 11 bird's eggs, 11 circles on box kite, 11 flowers, 11 kites, 11 leaves, 11 orange kite-tail bows, 11 piglets, 11 rays on sun, 11 segments on beehive, 11 squares on elephant's shorts, 11 stripes on piglet's shirt, 11 triangles on box kite

12: 12, 12 arms on 1 mannequin, 12 bunnies, 12 escalator steps, 12 flowers on dress, 12 hats, 12 keys on cash register, 12 lavender stripes on bear's skirt, 12 perfume bottles, 12 spotlights, 12 striped boxes, 12 windowpanes on first floor

13: 13, 13 animals on Ferris wheel, 13 balloons, 13 bananas, 13 darts, 13 spikes on iguana, 13 spots on giraffe, 13 stripes on gorilla's shirt, 13 teeth

14: 14, 14 blue books, 14 bookworms, 14 freckles, 14 green books, 14 open, falling books, 14 purple books, 14 red books, 14 triangles on boy's shirt

15: 15, 15 dots on bathing suit, 15 fans, 15 glasses, 15 ice cubes, 15 lizards, 15 mice, 15 red stripes on blow-up toy, 15 spikes on floating lizard's back, 15 straws, 15 towels

16: 16, 16 baseball bats, 16 baseballs, 16 bleacher banners, 16 fans, 16 hot dogs, 16 legs on pitcher, 16 spots on ladybug, 16 stadium lights, 16 yellow flags

17: 17, 17 coconuts on natives' heads, 17 eyelashes on female bird, 17 flowers on bracelets, 17 oranges on skirt, 17 parrots, 17 pieces of debris floating in ocean, 17 portholes, 17 tail feathers on green parrot, 17 tentacles on sea anemone, 17 trees

18: 18, 18 feathers on owl wing, 18 flowers, 18 geese, 18 leaves, 18 mouse whiskers, 18 prongs on antlers, 18 scouts, 18 snow-covered mountains

19: 19, 19 crescents on ape's shorts, 19 flowers in flower bed, 19 skateboards, 19 stripes on rabbit's shorts, 19 teeth on gorilla, 19 toes on frog, 19 windows on house

20: 20, 20 bird's eggs, 20 books, 20 dots on pajamas, 20 houses in valley, 20 mountains, 20 slats on shutter, 20 spots on owl, 20 stars, 20 stripes on tail